impact

3

Grammar Book

T0349582

NATIONAL GEOGRAPHIC
L E A R N I N G

Australia · Brazil · Mexico · Singapore · United Kingdom · United States

impact

3

Grammar Book

Question tags

Special uses of *it*

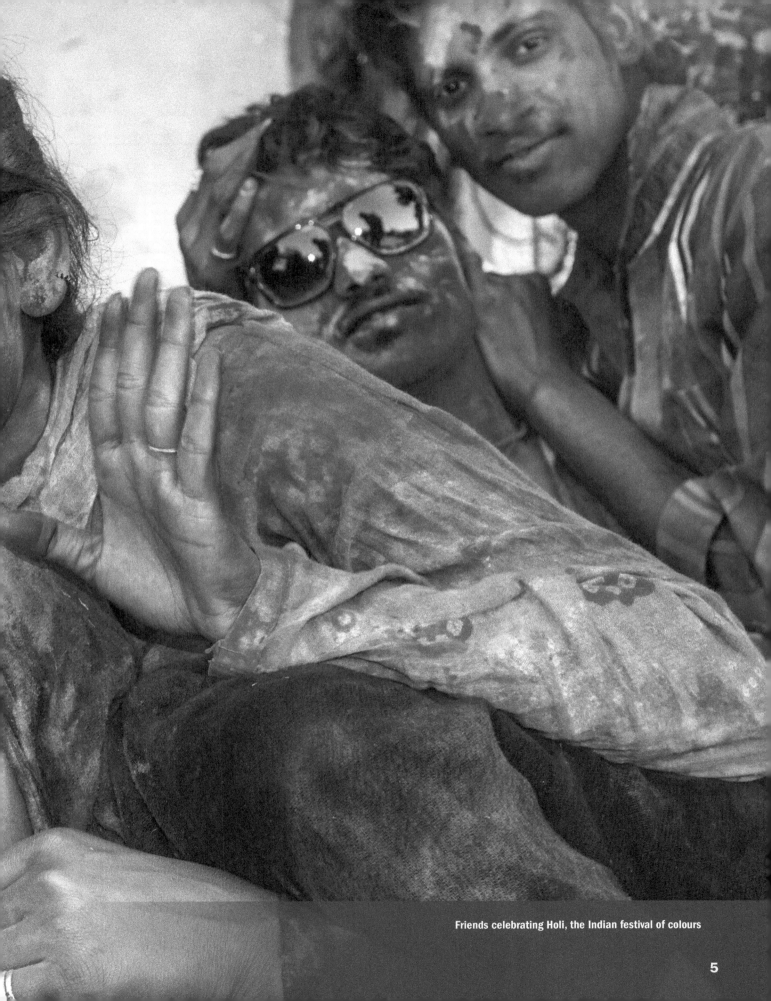

Friends celebrating Holi, the Indian festival of colours

Question tags are short questions at the end of statements. We use question tags:
- to confirm our opinion, or an idea.

*Alicia is friendly, **isn't she**?* (We are not sure if Alicia is friendly.)
- when we are seeking agreement.

*You're nervous about the competition, **aren't you**?* (We are fairly sure that the person is nervous.)

We make question tags with an auxiliary verb + a pronoun.

*David likes tennis, **doesn't he**?*

When the sentence is positive, we use a negative question tag.

*Lin also plays the flute, **doesn't she**?*

When the sentence is negative, we use a positive question tag.

*Rick doesn't live near here, **does he**?*

The question tag for *I am* is **aren't I**?

REMEMBER

We use our tone of voice to show if we are confirming our opinion or seeking agreement.

If the voice goes up at the end of the question, it is a genuine question, because we are not sure of the answer.

*You're not hungry, **are you**?*

If the voice goes down at the end of the question, we are asking the person to agree with us because we are fairly sure of the answer already.

*You're hungry, **aren't you**?*

We often use a negative sentence + a positive question tag to ask for things or information, or to ask someone to do something. The voice goes up in these questions.

*You couldn't make me a sandwich, **could you**?*

1 **Complete the sentences with *is*, *isn't*, *are* or *aren't*.**

Example: *You are a chef, **aren't** you?*

1. She isn't very well, _____ she?

2. I am so funny, _____ I?

3. We _____ going to miss the bus, aren't we?

4. He _____ joking, isn't he?

5. You _____ paying attention, aren't you?

6. They are a great band, _____ they?

7. It's a cold day, _____ it?

8. You are studying English, _____ you?

2 **Match the two parts to make questions.**

1. They didn't come to the party,
2. She didn't receive my invitation,
3. You will tell me about your trip,
4. I can phone her to apologise,
5. He won't leave without me,
6. She is very competitive,

a. won't you?
b. isn't she?
c. did they?
d. can't I?
e. did she?
f. will he?

3 **Complete the questions.**

Example: *I'm not* annoying you, am I?

1. _____ listening to me, was he?
2. _____ going to be in trouble, aren't they?
3. _____ finish the project by Monday, won't you?
4. _____ afford a new car, can we?
5. _____ like classical music, does he?
6. _____ cooked this dish very well, have they?
7. _____ starting to learn new techniques, isn't he?
8. _____ go out very often, do they?

4 **Use the prompts to write question tags.** Then write answers.

Example: *you / be / very bossy*
> *You're very bossy, aren't you?   No, I'm not!*

1. your friend / sometimes ignore / you

_____   _____

2. your dad / make / the best fish pie

_____   _____

3. Mr Lee / not like / Chinese food

_____   _____

4. your classmates / be / very competitive

_____   _____

5. you / live / near the sea

_____   _____

All sentences (except for commands) need a subject. We can use **it** in contexts where no other subject is present. We use **it** to talk about:

• the weather.

It's (It is) *cold outside.*

• distance.

It's *a half-mile walk from here. We're late!*

• the time, or to talk about the time of day.

It's *the middle of the night!*

• likes, dislikes and general opinions.

I love **it** *when she smiles.*

➲ See grammar box on page 52.

1 **Rewrite the sentences.** Start each new sentence with *It*.

Example: *The weather is wet.*

       It's raining.

1. The time is seven o'clock.

   _____

2. He's fallen off his bike. How awful!

   _____

3. The city is 20 minutes' drive away.

   _____

4. The weather is very windy today.

   _____

5. People interrupting me makes me angry.

   _____

6. When my friends don't answer the phone, I am annoyed.

   _____

7. There is snow falling.

   _____

8. The ridiculous thing is that I have forgotten my coat.

   _____

2 **Put the words in the correct order.**

Example: *when / we / to / the / cinema / go / happy / it / makes / me*
   It makes me happy when we go to the cinema.

1. warm / very / today / it / is

   _____

2. hot / in / the / desert / it / not / always / is

   _____

3. long / a / way / here? / from / is / it

   _____

4. win / I / it / first / love / prize / when / I

   _____

5. annoyed / I / am / that / it / is / not / often

   _____

6. that / drives / me / mad / it / don't / eat / people / healthily

   _____

7. like / it / I / when / kind / to / me / people / are

   _____

8. understand / it / I / don't / when / rude / people / to / others / are

   _____

3 **Complete the sentences with your own ideas.**

Example: *It is bad when **people throw litter on the beach**.*

1. It drives me crazy when _____.
2. I love it when _____.
3. It makes me annoyed when _____.
4. I hate it when _____.
5. It is _____.
6. It's a _____.
7. It's strange when _____.
8. It's unusual that _____.

WRITING

Write five questions which include *it*-phrases.

Example: ***It's** annoying when people interrupt you, isn't it?*

Modals

Infinitives with and without *to*

A Nile crocodile carrying its young

We use **could have**, **might have**, **may have**, **must have** + past participle to show how sure or certain we are about past situations.

We use **could have** or **might have** when we are not sure about what happened (or *why*, *how* or *when*, etc.).

*They cancelled their hiking plans. They **could have read** about that escaped bear.*

*He refuses to go in the water. He **might have seen** a jellyfish.*

We use **may have** when we are fairly sure about what happened.

*She won't get out of the car now. She **may have heard** the neighbour's dogs fighting.*

We use **must have** when we are very sure, or certain, about what happened.

*They took her to hospital immediately. That spider **must have been** poisonous.*

➔ See grammar box on page 52.

REMEMBER

Have does NOT change to *has* in the third person.
*It may **have** been poisonous!*
The modal changes in the negative, NOT the *auxiliary*.
*He **can't have** seen the spider.*

---

1 **Complete the conversation with the correct modal verb.**

A: Oh dear! I _____ may _____ have left my car keys in the house. (fairly sure)

B: You ¹_____ have taken them with you! (very sure)

A: I don't know! I ²_____ have left them in the car last night. But the car locks itself! (not sure)

B: Let's not panic yet. You ³_____ have dropped them on the ground. (not sure)

A: I ⁴_____ have dropped them. I would have heard that! (not sure)

B: You ⁵_____ have ... Let's look for them. (fairly sure)

A: I ⁶_____ have left them in my bag. (fairly sure)

B: Yes, you ⁷_____ have! They are not anywhere on the ground. (very sure)

A: Or I ⁸_____ have put them in the kitchen somewhere ... (not sure)

2 (Circle) the correct option.

Example: *My stomach hurts. I* (may) / *mustn't have eaten too much!*

1. My English book is not in my bag. I **could** / **might not** have packed it this morning.

2. The lesson was really boring. The teacher **could** / **must** have made it more fun!

3. My sister is going to a party tonight. She **could** / **may** have invited me!

4. I saw a man trip over. He **may** / **may not** have hurt himself.

5. I ate something which made me ill last night. It **could** / **couldn't** have been the fish.

6. It **couldn't** / **may** have been my husband on the train. He was with me all day!

7. Your ankle is very swollen. You **may** / **might not** have sprained it.

8. He **might** / **must** have said that already. I wasn't listening.

3 **Read the scenarios.** Decide what could/might/may/must have happened. Write sentences.

Example: *The dog has run away in the park.*
He may have seen a squirrel!

1. My little brother has a cut on his knee and is crying.

_____

2. My sister looks very tired this morning.

_____

3. My brother is laughing at the television.

_____

4. The fallen tree was blocking the road.

_____

5. The lion was sleeping in the shade of a tree.

_____

6. I thought I heard something under my bed last night.

_____

7. My parents are arguing in the front of the car.

_____

8. My mother was late home from work.

_____

We use the **infinitive with *to***:
- if the infinitive is the subject of the sentence.

To hold a rat is very scary.
- when verbs that express likes and dislikes are followed by an infinitive.

I like to collect insects.
- after common verbs such as *want, try, begin, continue, hope, forget* and *remember*.

I want to touch the spider.

The crocodile tried to bite me.

He forgot to feed his pet.
- after *to be* + adjective.

I'm sad to hear your news.

We use the **infinitive without *to***:
- after modal verbs.

You could try holding the snake.
- after verbs describing senses (*see, hear, feel*).

I heard the bird sing.
- with causative verbs (verbs which express cause).

He made me do it.
- with the verb *let*. We don't use *to*, but we must use an object.

They didn't let me drive their car.

The verb *help* can be used with or without *to*.

Can you help me (to) feed the spiders?

---

1 **Circle** the correct option.

Example: *I* (**eat**)/ *to eat fruit in the morning.*

1. We heard the lion **roar** / **to roar** at sunset.

2. They made me **touch** / **to touch** the snake. It was smooth, not slimy!

3. I promise **look after** / **to look after** you in the nature reserve.

4. I remembered **bring** / **to bring** some water on our jungle trek.

5. She didn't want **go** / **to go** diving yesterday.

6. I'll phone George and have him **collect** / **to collect** me from the station.

7. Oh dear. I forgot **pack** / **to pack** the phone charger.

8. That's definitely the place **visit** / **to visit**.

2 **Are these sentences correct?** Tick the correct sentences. Rewrite the incorrect sentences.

Example: *I can't wait see your new pet.*
> ***I can't wait to see your new pet.***

1. I really want see some wild animals.

   _____

2. Can I to touch the spider?

   _____

3. I'd love to visit a reptile house.

   _____

4. I saw a leopard to catch a gazelle.

   _____

5. He forgot shut the gate.

   _____

6. I hope we get the chance to see some sharks.

   _____

7. Did your mum let you buy the new cage for your snake?

   _____

8. Did they let you to take photos of it?

   _____

3 **Imagine you are going on holiday with your parents.** Complete these sentences with your own ideas.

Example: *Have you remembered **to pack your suitcase**?*

1. Mum, please don't make me _____!
2. You never let me _____!
3. When we get on the plane, I want _____.
4. My wish for this holiday is _____.
5. I can't believe I forgot _____!
6. Luckily, I remembered _____.
7. I can't wait _____.
8. _____ another night in this hotel would be terrible!

WRITING

Your friend has gone on holiday. You don't know where he/she has gone or what he/she is doing.
Write four suggestions about your friend. Try to include modals and infinitives with and without *to*.

Example: *I know he wanted **to swim** in a warm sea. He **might have gone** to Mexico.*

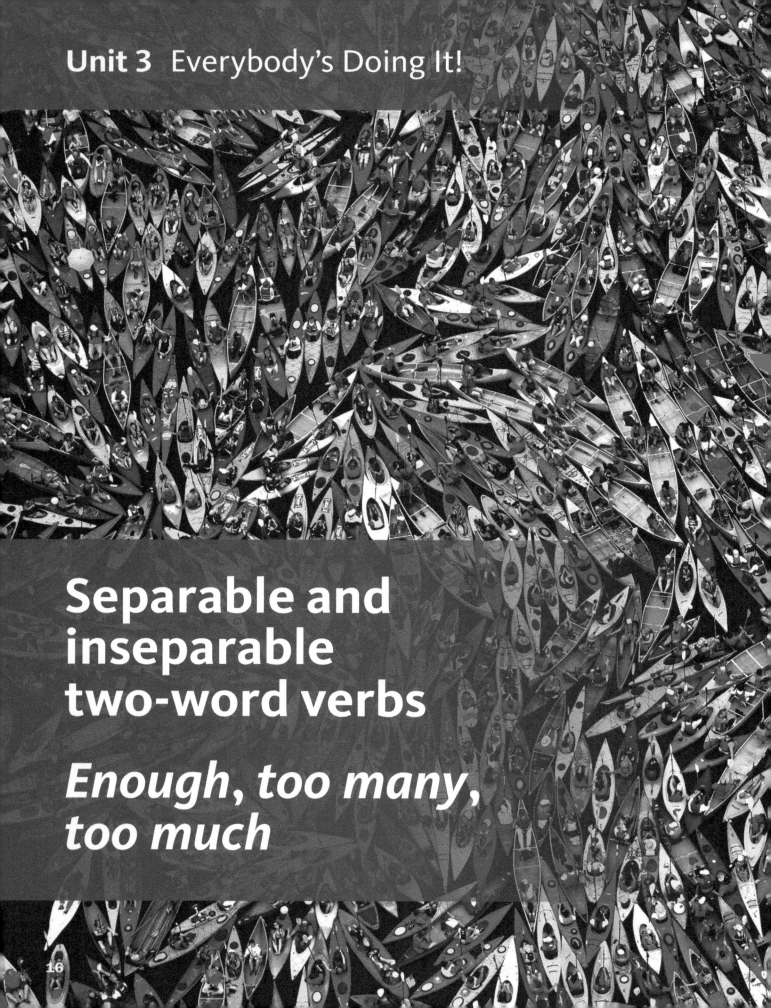

Separable and inseparable two-word verbs

Enough, too many, too much

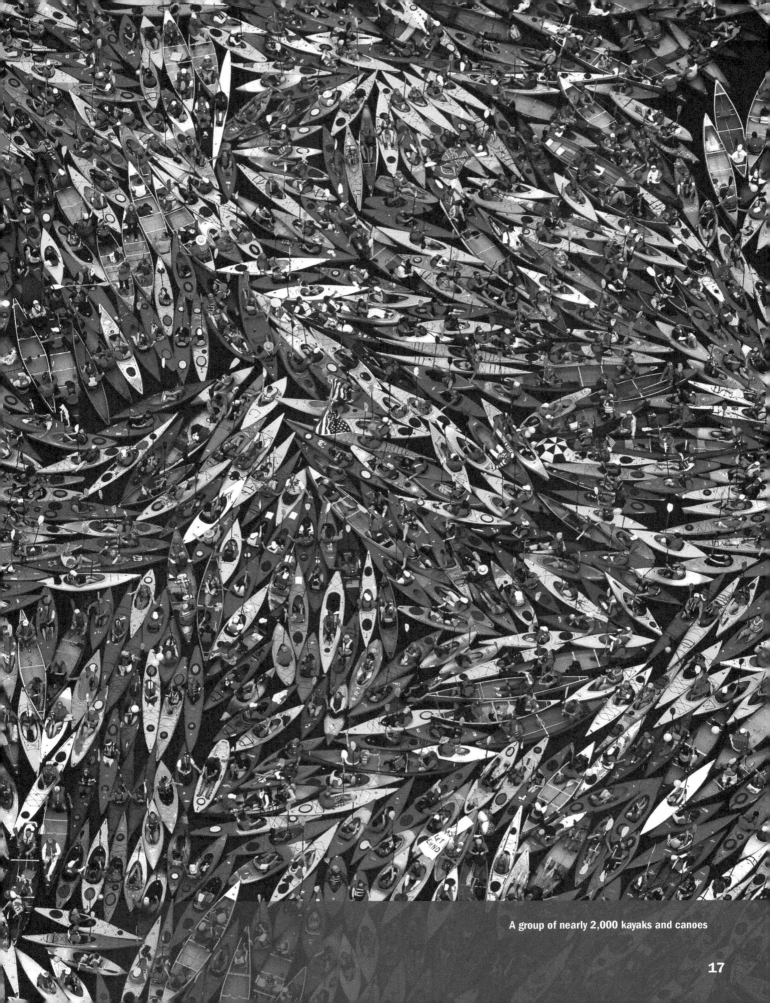

A group of nearly 2,000 kayaks and canoes

A simple way to understand two-word verbs is to put them in two groups: separable and inseparable verbs.

Separable verbs can be separated, or split, by the object of the verb.
*The scientists **talked over** the problem.* OR *The scientists **talked** the problem **over**.*
When the object of the verb is an object pronoun, it should always be separated.
*They **worked** it **out**.*
Phrasal verbs – usually a verb + adverb, e.g. *to throw away* – are separable.
*He **threw away** the packaging.* OR *He **threw** the packaging **away**.*

Inseparable verbs cannot be separated. The object (or object pronoun) can only go after the two words.
*The scientists **talked about** the problem. The scientists **talked about** <u>it</u>.*
*The scientists **looked into** the evidence. The scientists **looked into** <u>it</u>.*
Verbs followed by a preposition are inseparable. Common prepositions include: *after, at, for, with, into.*
*We **looked after** her dog for the weekend.* NOT *We **looked** her dog **after** for the weekend.*

➲ For lists of separable and inseparable verbs see Student's Book, page 149.

REMEMBER

There are always exceptions to rules! We can split some inseparable verbs with an adverb.
*The scientists **talked** <u>angrily</u> **about** the problem.*
*The scientists **looked** <u>carefully</u> **into** it.*

However, it is still more common to place the adverb at the end of the sentence.
*The scientists **talked about** the problem <u>angrily</u>.*
*The scientists **looked into** it <u>carefully</u>.*

However, this doesn't apply to all verbs!
*We **looked** <u>carefully</u> **after** her dog for the weekend.* ✘
*We **looked after** her dog <u>carefully</u> for the weekend.* ✔

1 **Complete the sentences with the two-word verbs in the box.** Make any necessary changes to the verbs.

| ~~break into~~ depend on | deal with | get over | go into | look for | listen to |

Example: *I lost my keys and had to* ***break into*** *my own house!*

1. It took you a long time to _____ your cold!

2. I won't _____ the details now.

3. Winning often _____ luck.

4. I am _____ a book by a Swedish author. Can you help me?

5. I enjoy _____ the radio when I am cooking.

6. You are _____ all your homework very well.

2 **Complete the sentences with the phrasal verbs in the box.** Make any necessary changes to the verbs.

| ~~bring up~~ cheer up | hand out | hold back | sort out | take off | work out |

Example: *My parents* ***brought*** *me* ***up*** *to be polite.*

1. This puzzle is tricky. Let's _____ it _____ together.

2. Please _____ your shoes _____ when you come in the house.

3. Her disability does not _____ her _____ at all!

4. Seeing your face always _____ me _____!

5. The neighbours _____ their differences _____ by talking to each other.

6. Please will you _____ the assignments _____ to the class?

3 **Are these sentences correct?** Tick the correct sentences. Rewrite the incorrect sentences.

Example: *Last night we ate at a restaurant out.*
   Last night we ate out at a restaurant.

1. Simon fell the hill down and hurt his shoulder. _____

2. He made the story up. It wasn't true. _____

3. Check out the waves! They're huge! _____

4. Yesterday, I ran my old head teacher into. _____

5. I don't really care olives for. _____

6. I grew in Italy up. _____

We use **enough** to talk about the right amount. **Enough** goes before nouns and after adjectives and adverbs.

*I've got **enough** pillows, but there are **not enough** feathers.*
*This coat is **not** big **enough** for me.*

We use **too many** and **too much** to talk about when there is more of something than is needed. We use **too many** with countable nouns and **too much** with uncountable nouns.
*You've put **too many** feathers in each pillow.*
*It's **too much** stress for me.*

1 **Complete the sentences with *too much* or *too many*.**

Example: *I have watched **too much** television today!*

1. We have got _____ work to do today.

2. They have _____ chores to do today.

3. I shouldn't eat _____ biscuits.

4. Yes, _____ sugar is bad for you!

5. I think I might have used _____ salt!

6. The teacher found _____ mistakes in your maths homework.

7. Let's try to finish the assignment today. It shouldn't take _____ time.

8. I have _____ clothes. I think I'll get rid of some.

2 **Circle the correct option.**

I haven't eaten (enough) / not enough food tonight!

1. Do you have **enough** / **not enough** people to help you, or do you need more?

2. There are **enough** / **not enough** people to make a team. We need to call some more.

3. There is **enough** / **not enough** fruit. I need to buy some more.

4. I don't have **enough** / **not enough** time to read the whole article.

5. Environmentalists say that **enough** / **not enough** effort is being made to save the rain forest.

6. Is **enough** / **not enough** being done to conserve endangered species?

7. Have you had **enough** / **not enough** to eat?

8. I can't believe you're still hungry! Is one ice cream **enough** / **not enough** for you?

3 **Are these sentences correct?** Tick the correct sentences. Rewrite the incorrect sentences.

Example: *You've given me too many money.*
        You've given me too much money.

1. There isn't enough time to catch the train.

   _____

2. There was too many music in the performance.

   _____

3. He didn't give me not enough advice.

   _____

4. I put too much oil in the pan.

   _____

5. Alex isn't enough tall to ride the rollercoaster.

   _____

6. We haven't got enough chair.

   _____

4 **Complete the paragraph with *enough, not enough, too many* or *too much*.**

When I went on holiday to Europe I thought I had taken _____*enough*_____ money for the trip.

In fact, I did have [1]_____ money, but I had taken [2]_____ dollars and

[3]_____ euros. There were [4]_____ times when the banks closed and I couldn't

exchange my dollars. I could have changed money at a bureau de change, but they charged

[5]_____ commission. But I learnt to plan ahead, so that I always had

[6]_____ money for a few days. Otherwise, the trip was amazing. There was

[7]_____ to see in only two weeks, and there was [8]_____ time to do everything

we wanted to. But I don't mind – it just means we have to plan another trip!

WRITING

Write a series of *Life Rules* for people in the 21st century. Use separable and inseparable verbs from this unit, as well as *enough, not enough, too many* and *too much*.

Example: *You can't have **too many** friends. They will always **cheer** you **up**. Use your gadgets, but don't **depend on** them. You can spend **too much** time on them if you're not careful!*

Present passive
Modals

Boys in São Paolo, Brazil

Present passive: Describing actions and processes

We often use the **present passive** to describe actions and processes.

They use a lot of pesticides to grow cotton. ⟶ A lot of pesticides **are used** to grow cotton.

They make clothing from synthetic materials. ⟶ Clothing **is made** from synthetic materials.

The passive is formed with *be* + past participle. We use the passive voice:

• to emphasise and focus on the action rather than the person who did it (the agent). The person doing the action is not important.

*These shoes **are manufactured** in Italy.*

• when we don't know who is doing the action.

*Seatbelts **are required** by law in all cars.*

• when it is easy to understand who is doing the action.

*More jeans **are bought** in the U.S. than anywhere else.*

The negative is formed by putting the word *not* after *be*.

*A lot of American clothing **is not made** in the U.S. any more.*

The objects in active sentences become the subjects in passive sentences.

Active sentences	Passive sentences
*Americans **buy** a lot of jeans.*	*A lot of jeans **are bought** by Americans.*
*They **make** excellent denim in Japan.*	*Excellent denim **is made** in Japan.*
*We mostly **use** blue dye in denim production.*	*Blue dye **is** mostly **used** in denim production.*
*Small mills **produce** limited edition jeans.*	*Limited edition jeans **are produced** in small mills.*
*America **grows** a lot of cotton.*	*A lot of cotton **is grown** in America.*

1 **Complete the paragraph with the verbs in the box.** Use the present passive.

~~manufacture~~	consider	develop	employ	export	make	use

Almost six million cars ___are manufactured___ in Germany every year. Many of these cars

¹_____ to countries around the world. German cars ²_____

to be reliable and well-made. The cars ³_____ in large factories in cities such as

Dresden. Around 750,000 people ⁴_____ in the car industry in Germany. A lot of new

technology ⁵_____ by German manufacturers. Sometimes, this technology

⁶_____ in racing cars as well as in road cars.

2 **Complete the sentences with the present passive of the verb in brackets.**

Example: *A lot of products* **aren't manufactured** *in the same countries they are sold. (not manufactured)*

1. A lot of the clothing _____ locally. (make)

2. Leather goods _____ in large factories, often in Asia. (produce)

3. Different labels _____ to the items. (attach)

4. The clothes _____ into shipping containers. (pack)

5. Stones _____ to create different designs and effects. (add)

6. The containers _____ to warehouses all over the world. (ship)

7. Sometimes, the clothing _____ if it is not up to standard. (reject)

8. Much of the world's cotton _____ in America. (grow)

3 **Rewrite the sentences in the present passive.**

Example: *People make some clothes from wool.*
     Some clothes are made from wool.

1. People weave fabric on a loom.

   _____

2. People draw new designs.

   _____

3. They use a lot of water to produce material.

   _____

4. They sell jeans all around the world.

   _____

5. Charity shops sell a lot of second-hand clothes.

   _____

6. Japan makes them.

   _____

7. They paint beautiful designs onto the silk.

   _____

8. People assemble the items in factories.

   _____

Modals: Making suggestions and giving advice about present and past actions

We use the modals **should** and **shouldn't**:

• to give advice.

*You **should be** more careful about reading labels.*

• to give a sense of obligation or duty.

*I **should do** my homework.*

• to ask for advice.

Should** I **buy that jacket?

We use the modals **could** and **couldn't**:

• to make suggestions.

*You **could reduce** your carbon footprint with a small change like this.*

• to ask if something is possible, or say that it is.

***Could** we **build** a house made entirely of recycled material? Yes, we **could**.*

• to ask for permission.

***Could** I **borrow** your pen?*

To talk about present actions, we use *should/could* + verb.

*You **shouldn't buy** that leather jacket.*

*You **could buy** that denim jacket.*

To talk about past actions, we use *should have/could have* + past participle.

*You **shouldn't have bought** that leather jacket.*

*You **could have bought** that denim jacket.*

1 **Complete the sentences with *could* or *could have* and the verb in brackets.**

Example: *Not buying fur **could help** wild animal populations. (help)*

1. You _____ your money instead of buying that new computer. (save)

2. Please _____ you _____ the clothes at 30˚? (wash)

3. We _____ less harmful detergent in our laundry. (use)

4. They _____ more to preserve the rain forest in the past. (do)

5. You _____ fewer clothes yesterday! (buy)

6. People _____ not to wear animal products. (choose)

7. We _____ the train instead of the car when we went to London. (take)

8. The last government _____ more laws to protect animals. (pass)

2 Complete the sentences with *should* or *should have* and the verb in brackets.

Example: *We **should have realised** that wearing fur was wrong.*

1. _____ we _____ environmentalists more carefully in the 60s? (listen to)

2. _____ we _____ animals to suffer? (allow)

3. We _____ fewer pesticides when we grow cotton. (use)

4. They _____ farm animals more space to move around. (give)

5. _____ you _____ that leather coat last week? (buy)

6. People _____ not to wear fur a long time ago. (choose)

7. We _____ our clothes unless they really need it. (not wash)

8. The hunters _____ that lion last year. (not kill)

3 Are these sentences correct? Tick the correct sentences. Rewrite the incorrect sentences.

Example: *Should you help me, please?*
   Could you help me, please?

1. Could fur farms be allowed these days?

   _____

2. This small change could really help.

   _____

3. You could be more careful when crossing the road.

   _____

4. Should you buy that coat last week?

   _____

5. Should we have planted the seeds by now?

   _____

6. I shouldn't have ate so much!

   _____

WRITING

Write your own rules and ideas about the environment. Use the present passive and *should* or *could*. Use your answers to Activity 1 to help you.

Example: *Fewer pesticides **should be used**.*

Past perfect

Past perfect continuous

Jetmen flying over the city of Dubai, United Arab Emirates

We use the **past perfect** (subject + *had/hadn't* + past participle):

• to refer to an action completed in the past before another action, event or moment in the past.
*Pterosaurs **had already disappeared** by the time modern birds evolved.*
*By the time humans tried to fly, the capability of flight **had developed** in four groups of animals.*

• in reported speech, when the speech being reported is in the present perfect.
*'I have flown in from New York,' she said. ⟶ She said she **had flown** in from New York.*

• to express an imaginary situation in an *if*-clause.
*If I **had grown** wings, I would not have got stuck in traffic!*

Note: *if*-clauses will be covered in Unit 6 and reported speech in Unit 7.

➜ See grammar box on page 52.

1 (Circle) **the correct option.**

Example: *My mum (had gone) / went to work by the time I got up.*

1. We **hadn't seen / haven't seen** the news but we heard it on the radio.

2. She **designs / had designed** the poster before she read the email.

3. I **had fell / had fallen** asleep before the programme finished.

4. They**'d never seen / 've never seen** a space capsule before they visited the museum.

5. I **wanted / had wanted** to help on the project, but they finished it before I arrived.

6. Our teacher wanted to know if we **have studied / had studied** for the exam.

7. My friend asked me if I **have borrowed / had borrowed** her dictionary.

8. He said he **had found / did find** my necklace.

2 **Write five sentences.** Use the past perfect forms of the verbs from the box.

| ~~eat~~ | visit | leave | go | fly | design |

Example: *I was invited for lunch but I said I **had** already **eaten**.*

1. _____

2. _____

3. _____

4. _____

5. _____

3 **Complete the sentences with the past perfect of the verb in brackets.**

Example: *The plane* **had left** *by the time we reached the airport. (leave)*

1. Humans _____ to fly long before the Wright brothers' successful flight in the 20th century. (try)

2. They _____ many different devices before they found a stable design. (built)

3. The Chinese _____ kites long before Marco Polo wrote about them. (invent)

4. Leonardo da Vinci _____ a long time studying flying objects before he designed his own machine. (spend)

5. He _____ his flying machine carefully but it still didn't fly. (design)

6. The Wright brothers _____ about flying since early childhood. (dream)

7. Pilots _____ to continue flying Concorde but it proved to be too expensive. (want)

8. It _____ possible for planes to fly faster than the speed of sound before jet engines. (not be)

4 **Change the statements from direct speech to reported speech.**

Example: *'I tried to call you,' said Sally.*
  Sally said she had tried to call you.

1. 'I've invented a flying machine,' said Leonardo da Vinci.

   _____

2. 'We've built a hot-air balloon,' said the Montgolfier brothers.

   _____

3. 'I've seen kites carrying men in China,' said Marco Polo.

   _____

4. 'We've flown a plane!' exclaimed the Wright Brothers.

   _____

5. 'We haven't flown very far,' they added.

   _____

6. 'I've flown faster than the speed of sound!' said Chuck Yeager.

   _____

7. 'I've designed a parachute,' said Fausto Veranzio.

   _____

8. 'We've landed on the moon,' said the astronauts.

   _____

Past perfect continuous: Talking about the first of two actions in the past

We use the **past perfect continuous** (subject + *had/hadn't* + *been* + present participle):
- to show that one action had been happening before another action in the past.

*Before Louis Bleriot first crossed the English Channel in an aeroplane in 1909, pilots **had been using** hot-air balloons.*

- to emphasise the length of time an action lasted for.

*The Wright brothers **had been working** on powered flight for several years before Wilbur Wright flew for 2 hours and 19 minutes in 1908.*

- to refer to an action in the past that was in progress but was interrupted by another action.

*I **had been watching** television for hours when suddenly I heard the telephone.*

➔ See grammar box on page 52.

REMEMBER

We often use *when, before, for* and *since* with the present perfect continuous.
*They'd been watching the news **when** the TV exploded.*
*Had they been waiting long **before** the plane took off?*
*I'd been trying to log on **for** hours.*
*The villagers had been asking for broadband **since** 2013.*

---

1 **Change the verbs to the past perfect continuous.**

Example: *I thought.*　**I had been thinking.**

1. We went.　_____

2. They played.　_____

3. You worried.　_____

4. She laughed.　_____

5. He cried.　_____

6. You worked.　_____

7. I watched.　_____

8. It developed.　_____

2 **Write sentences using the verbs from Activity 1.**

Example: *I had been thinking **about him when he suddenly arrived!***

1. _____
2. _____
3. _____
4. _____
5. _____
6. _____
7. _____
8. _____

3 **Complete the sentences using the past perfect continuous of the verb in brackets.**

Example: *Chuck Yeager **had been working** as a test pilot for eight years when he flew at Mach 2 in 1953. (work)*

1. Yeager _____ fighter planes for three years before he became a test pilot. (fly)

2. Two days before he broke the sound barrier, Yeager _____ a horse when he fell and broke two ribs. (ride)

3. Da Vinci _____ about flight for years before he built a flying machine. (think)

4. He _____ his machine for years before he showed it to anyone. (build)

5. He _____ engineering before he became a fighter pilot. (study)

6. They _____ to visit the exhibition before they read the good reviews. (not plan)

WRITING

Write sentences about the progress made by pioneers in flight over the centuries.

Use the past perfect and past perfect continuous.

Example: *Leonardo da Vinci **had been thinking** about flying since he **was** a child.*

Present and past conditionals

Adverbs

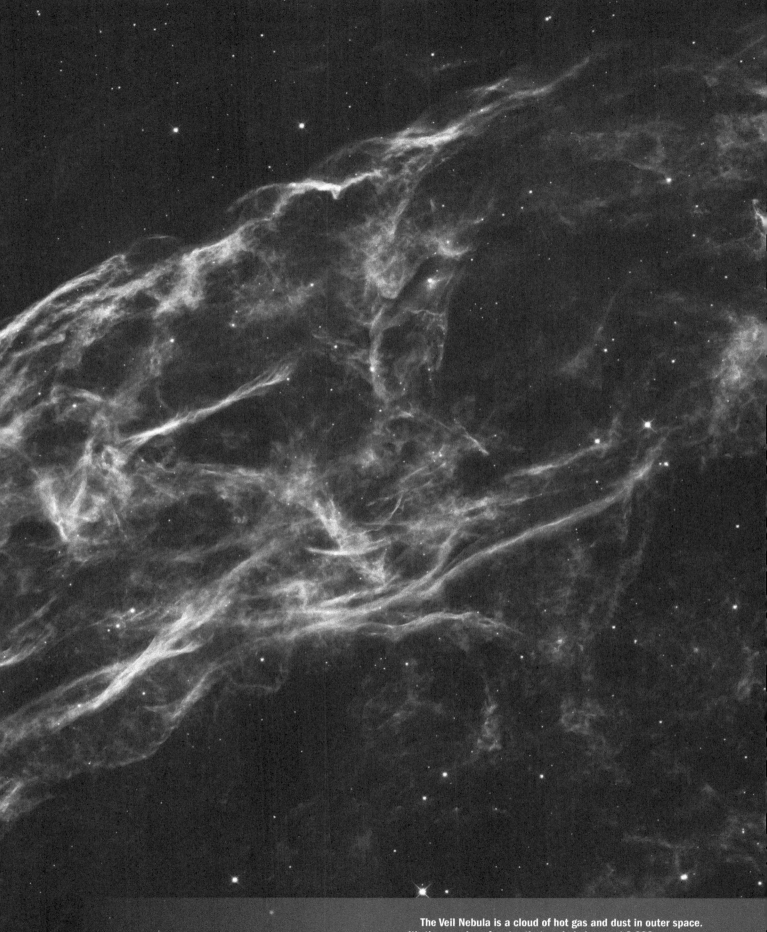

The Veil Nebula is a cloud of hot gas and dust in outer space.
It's the remains of a star that exploded around 8,000 years ago.

Present and past conditionals: Talking about unlikely (but possible) or impossible situations

This unit covers two types of conditional sentences (*if*-clauses): present (Type 2) and past (Type 3) conditional sentences.

We use Type 2 conditional sentences to talk about situations that are unlikely but possible to happen in the present or future.
*If I **were** a scientist, I **would focus** my research on Saturn.*
*He **would be** a space tourist if he **had** the money.*

To form the Type 2 conditional sentence we use:
- *if* + past simple, ***would/could/might*** + infinitive (without *to*)
*If I **knew** how to fly a plane, I **would apply** to be an astronaut.*

We use Type 3 conditional sentences to talk about impossible situations in the past (they have already happened).

To form the Type 3 conditional sentence we use:
- *if* + past perfect, ***would/could/might have*** + past participle
*If I **had been** alive in the 1950s, I **would have trained** to become an astronaut.*

The *if*-clause can go before or after the main clause. When the sentence begins with the *if*-clause, use a comma. When the sentence starts with the main clause, don't use a comma.
*If there **were** tours into space, I would visit Mars.*
*I would visit Mars if there **were** tours into space.*

1 **Complete the Type 2 conditional sentences.** Use the verbs in the box.

be	find	get	know	leave	live	~~have~~	not miss	spend

Example: *I would buy a plane if I **had** enough money.*

1. If I _____ good at maths, I would become an astronaut.

2. If you _____ more time in France, you would learn French more quickly.

3. His father would be very angry if he _____ what he'd done.

4. If I _____ near the sea, I would want to own a boat.

5. I wouldn't go into space even if I _____ the chance.

6. If she _____ so many training sessions, she would be in the team.

7. What would you do if you _____ some money in the street?

8. If they _____ earlier, they wouldn't be late for school.

2 **Match the two halves to make complete sentences.**

1. If I had been a NASA scientist in the 1960s,

2. I would have loved to have flown on an Apollo mission

3. The US wouldn't have gone to the moon

4. If they hadn't been so determined to succeed,

5. If the Soviets had reached the moon first,

6. We would invest in more space programmes

a. if I had been an astronaut in the 1960s.

b. it would have been seen as a humiliation for the US.

c. it would have been so exciting.

d. if the cost wasn't so high.

e. if they hadn't been competing with the Soviet Union.

f. they would never have landed on the moon.

3 **Complete the sentences.** Write the verb in brackets in the correct tense.

Example: *If I **were** rich, I would give my money to good causes. (be)*

1. If we _____ more money in space travel, we would want to study Mars. (invest)

2. If I knew her telephone number, I _____ her. (call)

3. I would travel to Australia if I _____ more time. (have)

4. If I were old enough to fly a plane, I _____ to fly a jumbo jet. (want)

5. If it wasn't raining outside, I _____ for a walk. (go)

6. If I had gone to university, I _____ engineering. (study)

7. I would have been frightened if I _____ the earthquake. (feel)

8. If I had known about the eclipse, I _____ to the cinema! (not go)

4 **Complete the sentences with *would/could/might have* + past participle.** Use your own ideas.

Example: *If I had been born 40 years earlier, **I would have been an explorer**.*

1. If I had lived in the 18th century, _____.

2. If we had listened in science class, _____.

3. If I had learnt how to play the guitar, _____.

4. If we had not turned right at the junction, _____.

5. If they had not invented the wheel, _____.

6. If I had had more time, _____.

7. If you and I had known each other five years ago, _____.

8. If we hadn't learnt Chinese, _____.

Adverbs describe verbs.

*The new satellite transmits data **efficiently**.*

Regular adverbs are formed by adding *-ly* to the end of the adjective.

slow ⟶ *slowly*

quick ⟶ *quickly*

Irregular adverbs do not take *-ly*.

good ⟶ *well*

fast ⟶ *fast*

When we want to make comparative statements about how things are done, we use the same structures for adverbs as we use for comparative and superlative adjectives.

• *as ... as*

*The last satellite didn't transmit data **as efficiently as** the new satellite.*

• *more ... than*

*The new satellite transmits data **more efficiently than** the last satellite.*

• *less ... than*

*The last satellite transmitted data **less efficiently than** the new satellite.*

• *the most ...*

*The new satellite transmits data **the most efficiently** of all the satellites.*

When the irregular adverb is the same as the adjective, the comparative and superlative form remains the same.

*The new rover travels **fast**.*

*The last rover didn't travel **as fast as** the new rover.*

*The new rover travels **faster than** the last rover.*

*The new rover travels **the fastest** of all the rovers.*

➔ See irregular verbs list on page 54.

---

1 **Match the comparative adverbs.**

1. not as tall as
2. faster than
3. earlier than
4. harder than
5. not as accurately as
6. not as well as

a. less precisely than
b. not as slowly as
c. worse than
d. shorter than
e. not as easy as
f. not as late as

2 **Complete the sentences with the superlative form of the adverb.**

Example: *Planes fly faster than helicopters, but rockets fly **the fastest**.*

1. Hand-held telescopes are clearer than binoculars, but commercial telescopes are _____.

2. I understand robots better than my brother, but my sister understands them _____.

3. I eat more than my parents, but my brother eats _____.

4. My brother arrived home later than me, but my parents arrived _____.

5. The helicopter flies higher than the hot-air balloon, but the jet flies _____.

6. Lions are faster cats than leopards, but cheetahs are _____.

3 **Complete the second sentence so that it has the same meaning as the first.**

Example: *Jet planes don't travel as fast as rockets.*
   *Jet planes travel **more slowly than rockets**.*

1. Old engines work less efficiently than new ones.

   New engines work _____.

2. Jet engines work more reliably than diesel engines.

   Diesel engines don't work _____.

3. He explained things less clearly than I wanted.

   He didn't explain things _____.

4. She did not speak Spanish as fluently as me.

   She spoke Spanish _____.

5. I did not arrive as late as I thought I would.

   I arrived _____.

6. We fell asleep more slowly than the night before.

   We didn't fall asleep _____.

4 **Make comparative sentences with the adverbs.** Use your own ideas.

Example: *(slowest)*   ***Walking is not always the slowest way to get around a city.***

1. (faster)   _____

2. (clearly)   _____

3. (less reliably)   _____

4. (the most efficiently)   _____

5. (more accurately)   _____

6. (longer)   _____

Past passive

Reported speech

A museum worker moves *La Bella Principessa*, which many believe was painted by Leonardo da Vinci.

The **past passive** has a similar structure to the present passive (see Unit 4).

To form the past passive we use: *was/were* + past participle.

*Paint **was** usually **made** by mixing colours with oils.*

We use the passive to emphasise an action rather than the person who performed the action (the agent). However, when we use the past passive, it is common to focus more on the agent performing the action, especially when talking about artwork, buildings or discoveries. We do this by using *by*.

*Many different styles **were explored** by painters.*

The past passive is more common in written language, especially in academic texts.

The negative is formed by putting the word *not* after the auxiliary verb.

*Sometimes, artworks signed by an artist **were not painted** entirely by them, but with the help of assistants.*

→ See grammar box on page 53.

REMEMBER

We use the verb *be* as the auxiliary in all passive tenses. In the past passive, we use:

• *was* for singular subjects.

*The changing light during the day **was captured** by Monet.*

• *were* for plural subjects.

*Different colours **were favoured** by different artists.*

1 **Complete the sentences with the past passive of the verb in brackets.**

Example: *Paintings **weren't** always **displayed** in museums. (not displayed)*

1. The Ashmolean Museum in Oxford _____ in the late 1600s. (establish)

2. Before museums, most artworks _____ in private homes and palaces. (show)

3. Artists _____ busy by rich patrons. (keep)

4. Their work _____ by rich people. (buy)

5. Originally, they _____ to develop new styles. (not encourage)

6. Impressionist art _____ by many people at first. (not appreciated)

2 **Rewrite the sentences in the past passive so that the meaning is the same.**

Example: *Artists mixed colours on a palette.*
 Colours were mixed on a palette (by artists).

1. Assistants helped many artists in their studios.

   _____

2. People painted cave paintings.

   _____

3. Da Vinci sketched out his inventions.

   _____

4. The researchers recorded the data.

   _____

5. Pablo Picasso completed *Guernica* in June 1937.

   _____

6. He painted it as a protest against the town's destruction.

   _____

7. He first exhibited it at the Paris International Exhibition in 1937.

   _____

8. Sometimes, people don't understand abstract art.

   _____

3 **Read.** Answer the questions in full sentences using the past passive.

Diego Velázquez was the leading artist of the Spanish Golden Age. He was the official artist at the court of King Philip IV of Spain. He completed his most famous work, *Las Meninas*, in 1656. The figures he painted were the daughter of the king, Margarita Teresa, and her ladies-in-waiting. Behind them, Velázquez portrayed himself working at a large canvas. The king and queen themselves were depicted in a mirror in the background. The king was very happy with the painting, possibly because it was painted from his perspective. He kept it hanging in his private quarters for the rest of his life. The royal family passed it to the Prado museum when it opened in 1819.

Example: *Who employed Diego Velázquez?*
 Diego Velázquez (He) was employed by the court of King Philip IV of Spain.

1. When was *Las Meninas* completed?   _____

2. Was the king's daughter shown in the painting? _____

3. Was Velázquez included in the painting?   _____

4. Where was the painting first hung?   _____

5. Where was the painting moved to in 1819?   _____

We use **reported speech** (indirect speech) when we tell someone else what another person said. We don't use the speaker's exact words or use quotation marks.

We use reported speech to tell someone else:
- something that is being said now.

'I'm drawing a tree.'   ⟶   *He says he is drawing a tree.*

- something that was said in the past.

'I'm drawing a tree.'   ⟶   *He said he was drawing a tree.*

Generally, reported speech, unless it is reported immediately, involves a change in tense between the direct speech and the reported speech.

present	**past**
will ⟶	*would*
'I will save my money,' she said.	*She said she **would** save her money.*
can ⟶	*could*
'Can I borrow your pencil?' he asked.	*He asked if he **could** borrow my pencil.*
must ⟶	*had to*
'I must find the address,' she said.	*She said she **had to** find the address.*

➲ See grammar box on page 53.

REMEMBER

Change the pronoun in reported speech to show the speaker's point of view.

*'Can **I** borrow **your** pen?'*   ⟶   *He asked if **he** could borrow **my** pen.*

When reporting commands, use *told* + person + the infinitive with *to*.

'Go to bed!' said Mum.   ⟶   *Mum **told me to go** to bed.*

WRITING

Write sentences of reported speech with the past passive.

Example: *'Van Gogh's Sunflower series was painted in 1888–9,' said the guide.*

    The guide said that Van Gogh's Sunflower series had been painted in 1888–9.

1. 'People didn't consider him a great artist during his lifetime,' said the guide.

2. 'He gave one of the early *Sunflower* paintings to Gauguin,' the guide added.

3. 'I don't think it was painted especially for him,' said the guide.

4. 'The artist's genius was not understood by his contemporaries,' added the guide.

1 **Rewrite the statements as reported speech.** Pay attention to the changes in the tense and the pronoun.

Example: *'We are painting a seascape,' he said.*
       He said they were painting a seascape.

1. 'I like to sketch on an iPad,' she said.

   _____

2. 'I prefer to use watercolours,' I replied.

   _____

3. 'It takes me a long time to finish a painting,' said the artist.

   _____

4. 'I love going to art galleries,' he said.

   _____

5. 'I really enjoy fishing,' my grandfather said.

   _____

6. 'It's great to be outside,' he added.

   _____

7. 'I don't like going to museums,' he said.

   _____

8. 'I visited the Louvre last weekend,' she said.

   _____

2 **Complete the reported sentences with the correct tense and pronoun.**

Example: *'You will have a test in your next lesson,' my teacher said.*
       My teacher said **we would have** *a test in our next lesson.*

1. 'I'll make a picnic for lunch,' said my grandfather.

   My grandfather said _____ a picnic for lunch.

2. 'You can take a photo and copy it,' said the artist.

   The artist told _____ a photo and copy it.

3. 'Can you meet me by the river?' asked Emil.

   Emil asked if _____ by the river.

4. 'Do you like my painting? she asked.

   She asked me if _____ painting.

5. 'I've been waiting for you for ages,' said Pete.

   Pete said _____ for ages.

6. 'You can borrow my laptop,' said her brother.

   Her brother said _____ laptop.

Gerunds and infinitives
Sense verbs + infinitive

A performer breakdancing in a cloud of coloured smoke

Gerunds are verbs with the *-ing* ending.
dancing   studying   learning
A gerund is a verb that acts like a noun. It can be used wherever a noun can be used, as the subject or object of a sentence, and after a preposition.
***Dancing** is a popular form of self-expression.* (subject)
***Learning music** is important.* (object)
*I'm interested in **acting** as a career.* (after a preposition)

Some verbs used to express opinion can be followed by either an infinitive with *to* or a gerund.
Verbs: *like, love, hate, prefer*
*I love **singing** on stage.* OR *I love **to sing** on stage.*

Some verbs cannot be followed by an infinitive, only a gerund.
Verbs: *admit, be used to, deny, can't help, can't stand, dislike, (don't) mind, enjoy, feel like, finish, imagine, keep, miss, practise, spend time*
*I practised **playing** the whole piece before the concert.*

Gerunds can also go after the verb *go* when talking about activities.
*I want to go **running** later.*

The **infinitive** with *to* is also used to express purpose.
*I sent her a text message (in order) **to invite** her to the performance.*

The infinitive with *to* can follow adjectives.
*She was sad **to miss** the performance.*

1 (Circle) the correct option.

Example: *I can't afford **going** / (**to go**) to the theatre.*

1. I decided **buying** / **to buy** a new mobile phone.

2. I can't help **liking** / **to like** some graffiti.

3. Can you keep **sending** / **to send** me your photos?

4. You should consider **going** / **to go** to art college.

5. He pretended **knowing** / **to know** a lot about the painting.

6. They offered **painting** / **to paint** the house.

7. I couldn't resist **visiting** / **to visit** the museum again.

8. They convinced me **trying** / **to try** pottery.

2 Rewrite the sentences using a gerund.

Example: *I love to perform plays with my friends.*
   I love performing plays with my friends.

1. I hate to listen to my sister singing.

   _____

2. Some people like to watch living statues.

   _____

3. I would hate to stand still for so long.

   _____

4. We love to watch the sunset.

   _____

5. I love to act in my sister's videos.

   _____

6. We prefer to sing in a choir instead of doing solos.

   _____

3 Complete the sentences using the gerund or infinitive with *to* of the verb in brackets. Use your own ideas.

Example: *It would surprise me **to see a living statue fall over**. (see)*

1. I expected _____. (find)
2. I really love _____. (act)
3. I mostly enjoy _____. (sing)
4. I continue _____. (enjoy)
5. I can't stand _____. (hear)
6. I challenged him _____. (try)
7. I usually prefer _____. (go)
8. I often like _____. (listen to)

WRITING

Write five sentences about your own performing, cultural and artistic habits, likes and dislikes.
Use a mixture of gerunds and infinitives.

Example: *I like **to go** to the cinema, but I don't like **going** every day.*

Verbs referring to the senses (*see*, *hear*, *feel*, etc.) can be followed by:
- an object + the infinitive without *to*

*Did you **see the band perform** in concert?*
- an object + a present participle *(-ing)*

*Did you **see the band performing** in concert?*

When sense verbs are followed by a present participle, there's a little more focus on the action in progress. Most people, however, use the two patterns interchangeably.

*Come on! Let's watch the DJ **spin** records.*

*Come on! Let's watch the DJ **spinning** records.*

The present participle is formed by adding *-ing* to the infinitive. If the infinitive ends in an *e*, it is removed.

talk ⟶ *talking*

rise ⟶ *rising*

REMEMBER

The present participle has the same form as the gerund, but it cannot be used as a noun. It can be used as an adjective, however.

*I enjoyed the **rising** chorus at the end.*

1 **Complete the sentences with a sense verb from the box.**

| feel | hear | listen to | see | smell | ~~watch~~ |

Example: *They **watched** their team win the final last night.*

1. She _____ her neighbour scream and went to find out what happened.

2. Did you _____ the house shake during the earthquake?

3. We _____ the cake burning and remembered we'd left it in the oven.

4. We didn't _____ him fall over on the ice because we were still inside the house.

5. I _____ the lecturer explain the process, but I didn't understand it all.

2 (Circle) the correct sense verb.

Example: I (heard) / felt the choir perform in the concert last night.

1. Did you **feel** / **see** the wind blowing! It was really strong.

2. I **heard** / **watched** the thunder roaring in the night.

3. I didn't **see** / **feel** them performing last night. Were they good?

4. I **watched** / **looked** her playing football.

5. Did you **hear** / **sound** her singing?

6. I **felt** / **heard** him touch my arm.

3 Write sentences using the prompts.

Example: love / hear / fireworks / explode
    I love hearing the fireworks explode.

1. love / feel / wind / blow

_____

2. hate / smell / fire / burn

_____

3. like / see / deer / jump

_____

4. enjoy / watch / dancers / move

_____

5. prefer / listen to / flutes / play

_____

6. not like / hear / people / shout

_____

4 Complete the sentences with the verbs in the box.

| bang | burn | climb | draw | ~~play~~ | run | talk |

Example: I haven't heard them **play/playing** that song before.

1. Did you see them _____ down the road?

2. I was able to hear the people _____, even though they were in the next room.

3. I heard him _____ his drums all night.

4. Did you see the thief _____ over the wall?

5. I felt the hot tea _____ my mouth.

6. We watched the artist _____ the cartoon.

Grammar boxes

Unit 1 Special uses of *it*

Structures with *it*	
It + *to be* + adjective + clause	*It's strange that we've had so much rain.*
Subject + verb + *it* + *when*-clause.	*I hate **it** when the alarm goes off.*
It + verb + object pronoun + adjective + *when*-clause.	*It drives me crazy when I have to hurry.*
It + *to be* + adjective + infinitive.	*It is strange to think that the town has been flooded.*

Unit 2 Modals

	Affirmative	Negative	Question	Short answers
I / You / He / She / It / We / They	must have seen	mustn't (must not) have seen	Must ... have seen ...?	Yes, ... must. No, ... mustn't.

Unit 4 Modals

	Affirmative	Negative	Question	Short answers
I / You / He / She / It / We / They	could/should	couldn't (could not)/shouldn't (should not)	Could/Should ...?	Yes, ... could/ should. No, ... couldn't/ shouldn't.

Unit 5 Past perfect

	Affirmative	Negative	Question	Short answers
I / You / He / She / It / We / They	had flown	hadn't (had not) flown	Had ... flown?	Yes, ... had. No, ... hadn't.

Unit 5 Past perfect continuous

	Affirmative	Negative	Question	Short answers
I / You / He / She / It / We / They	had been watching	hadn't (had not) been watching	Had ... been watching?	Yes, ... had. No, ... hadn't.

Unit 7 Past passive

Verb	Active sentence	Past passive sentence
to explore	Painters *explored* many different styles.	Many different styles *were explored* (by painters).
to make	Artists *made* paint by mixing colours with oil.	Paint *was made* by mixing colours with oil.
to develop	Artists *developed* different techniques.	Different techniques *were developed* (by artists).
to create	Goya *created* many of his works at night.	Many of Goya's works *were created* at night.

Unit 7 Reported speech

Direct speech	Reported speech
Present simple *'I paint landscapes,' he said.*	Past simple *He said he painted landscapes.*
Present continuous *'I am reading a book,' she said.*	Past continuous *She said she was reading a book.*
Past simple *'I sculpted a statue,' said John.*	Past perfect simple *John said he had sculpted a statue.*
Past continuous *'I was working on a painting,' she said.*	Past perfect continuous *She said she had been working on a painting.*
Present perfect simple *'I have drawn a sketch,' said Ann.*	Past perfect simple *Ann said she had drawn a sketch.*
Present perfect continuous *'I've been sketching for hours,' he said.*	Past perfect continuous *He said he had been sketching for hours.*
Will *'I will show you later,' he said.*	*Would* *He said he would show me later.*
Can *'I can paint with oils,' said Tim.*	*Could* *Tim said he could paint with oils.*
Must *'I must finish the sketch soon,' he said.*	*Had to* *He said he had to finish the sketch soon.*

Irregular verbs

Infinitive	Past simple	Past participle	Infinitive	Past simple	Past participle
be	were	been	leave	left	left
beat	beat	beaten	lend	lent	lent
become	became	become	let	let	let
begin	began	begun	lie (down)	lay	lain
bend	bent	bent	light	lit	lit
bet	bet	bet	lose	lost	lost
bite	bit	bitten	make	made	made
bleed	bled	bled	mean	meant	meant
blow	blew	blown	meet	met	met
break	broke	broken	overcome	overcame	overcome
bring	brought	brought	pay	paid	paid
build	built	built	put	put	put
burn	burnt	burnt	quit	quit	quit
buy	bought	bought	read	read	read
carry	carried	carried	ride	rode	ridden
catch	caught	caught	ring	rang	rung
choose	chose	chosen	rise	rose	risen
come	came	come	run	ran	run
cost	cost	cost	say	said	said
cut	cut	cut	see	saw	seen
deal	dealt	dealt	sell	sold	sold
dig	dug	dug	send	sent	sent
dive	dived	dived	set	set	set
do	did	done	sew	sewed	sewn
draw	drew	drawn	shake	shook	shaken
drink	drank	drunk	shine	shone	shone
drive	drove	driven	show	showed	shown
dry	dried	dried	shrink	shrank	shrunk
eat	ate	eaten	shut	shut	shut
fall	fell	fallen	sing	sang	sung
feed	fed	fed	sink	sank	sunk
feel	felt	felt	sit	sat	sat
fight	fought	fought	sleep	slept	slept
find	found	found	slide	slid	slid
flee	fled	fled	speak	spoke	spoken
fly	flew	flown	spend	spent	spent
forbid	forbade	forbidden	spin	spun	spun
forget	forgot	forgotten	stand	stood	stood
forgive	forgave	forgiven	steal	stole	stolen
freeze	froze	frozen	stick	stuck	stuck
fry	fried	fried	sting	stung	stung
get	got	got	stink	stank	stunk
give	gave	given	strike	struck	struck
go	went	gone	swear	swore	sworn
grind	ground	ground	sweep	swept	swept
grow	grew	grown	swim	swam	swum
hang	hung	hung	swing	swung	swung
have	had	had	take	took	taken
hear	heard	heard	teach	taught	taught
hide	hid	hidden	tear	tore	torn
hit	hit	hit	tell	told	told
hold	held	held	think	thought	thought
hurt	hurt	hurt	throw	threw	thrown
keep	kept	kept	understand	understood	understood
kneel	knelt	knelt	wake	woke	woken
knit	knitted	knitted	wear	wore	worn
know	knew	known	weave	wove	woven
lay	laid	laid	win	won	won
lead	led	led	write	wrote	written

NOTES

NOTES